Explaining
The Christian Faith

Answers To Questions Of Life

David Fardouly

Sovereign World

Scripture quotations are taken from the Holy Bible, New International
Version, copyright © 1973, 1978. International Bible Society. Published by
Hodder & Stoughton.

British Library Cataloguing in Publication Data
Fardouly, David
    Explaining the Christian Faith.
    1. Christianity
    I. Title
    230

    ISBN: 1 85240 068 4

SOVEREIGN WORLD LIMITED
P.O. Box 777, Tonbridge, Kent TN11 9XT, England.

Printed in the UK by Sussex Litho Ltd, Chichester, West Sussex.

Contents

Introduction

Have you ever wondered whether there is more to everyday life than just living? Is life only about working, sleeping, eating, and the occasional time when we really enjoy ourselves? Or is there something more?

For many people, life is about doing the right thing by their families, keeping the law and being basically 'good citizens'. Other people see the most important thing as being their contribution to the common good. Still others, who are perhaps less 'noble', believe that life is there to enjoy while it lasts. They have the attitude, 'Eat, drink, and be merry, for tomorrow we die!'

The truth is, though, that for most people, life just does not make sense! They live in a world where one person works hard and gets nothing, while another does nothing and yet has everything he or she could possibly want. On a global level, extreme poverty sits side by side with excessive self-indulgence. On a personal level, many people feel that they spend their lives working just to maintain what they have.

Something is wrong! Something is missing! There has to be more to life than what we see. Most people know this deep down, but they do not know where to look, who to trust, or what to do in order to get the answers they need.

Have you ever wondered whether there is a God? Does God seem so remote that you think He cannot possibly be interested in your life, even if He does exist? Maybe you want to know more, but you have been put off by the multitude of religions, all claiming to know the true way to God or enlightenment. Have you wondered why so many people get involved in religion, not just as a hobby, but as a lifestyle! If there is a God, which religion is the right one to follow?

Who was Jesus Christ? Do you know that Jesus Christ existed as an historical figure? He was written about by people who were not Christians, but who were alive at the same time as He was. Do you know who Jesus claimed to be? Do you know what Christians believe Jesus did for every person who has ever lived?

Most people don't like or want to ask such questions, because they are troubled by them—there's enough in life to worry about as it is! They feel that some things are simply beyond their understanding and so are best left alone. They just want to get on with life, enjoying what there is to enjoy, and hoping that they 'get it right'. These people sweep questions about life aside and get busy doing something else. They hope that the doubts will disappear or at least be forgotten for a time. The trouble is that all that seems to disappear is time itself!

It often takes a tragedy like death, an illness, or some other serious problem to knock us out of our complacent attitude to life, but isn't it important to find out the answers to these questions before it's too late? After all, we only have a limited time in which to do it! Is life just a senseless joke? What is life all about?

This book has been written to help you answer some of the questions you may have about life in general and Christianity in particular. If there is one question that has particularly troubled you, then look up the glossary of questions at the back of the book. This will show you where in the book your question has been answered. The 'Suggested Further Reading' list at the back of the book may also be of help to you.

1

What Are The Alternatives?

Are people looking for something?

People are searching for some meaning to life, of that there can be no doubt! Most of us want life to make sense and to have some form of purpose, but are we willing to take the time to discover that purpose?

Do we act like human ostriches?

Apparently ostriches don't actually bury their heads in the sand, they simply lay their heads on top of it. People, though, are not so smart! We do seem to make a habit of burying our heads in the sand. Often, we don't want to face the big issues, so instead of tackling them, we try to forget about them and hope they will go away. Unfortunately, they don't, and neither can we ignore questions about the purpose of life.

What are the main alternatives?

Most people would say that they haven't got the time to think about life and its meaning. They are far too busy studying, working, making money or trying to enjoy themselves. Everybody hopes for personal fulfilment. Some people try to find it by burying themselves in their work or study; others want power and seek satisfaction in extending their influence; still others strive for riches, believing that money will provide them with everything they need to really enjoy life. Many other people live only to enjoy themselves. They want one pleasure experience after another. But it seems that however successful people are in achieving these basically self-centred goals, they are still looking for something more.

On the other hand, some people try hard to find purpose in life by getting involved in charity work, or by doing the right thing to other people. Others work all their lives to improve the lot of humankind. These things are very noble, but they do not fill the emptiness within us all. The truth is that these activities only succeed in covering over that emptiness for a time.

Another group of people worthy of mention are those who wipe out their ability to reason or think. They use drugs, alcohol or meditation in order to gain an artificial sense of well-being. The trouble here is that it always wears off and they are left with the same old problems and difficulties.

Is this all there is?

Do you feel fulfilled in your life, or do you feel empty and know that something is missing? Have you ever thought, or even hoped, that there is something after your time on earth? Or do you believe that death is the end of you? Perhaps you feel that there has got to be something more, something better than what you have!

Isn't it sensible to try and tackle the deep questions of life now? Shouldn't you make an effort to discover the truth? Shouldn't you find out if there is a God? And if there is, shouldn't you find out if there is anything He wants you to do?

What is life all about?

2

If There Is A God, Which Religion Is Right?

Is there a God?

Scientists have discovered many of the laws which govern electricity, but they still cannot really define it. However, we know it exists, because we see the manifestations of it in our homes and places of work, etc. The same is true for the wind and even for the feelings that we have for one another. Similarly, we may not be able to see God and define Him, but we can know that He exists by the manifestations of Him that we see everywhere around us and by the feelings within us.

Throughout history, people of all civilisations have had their objects of worship—their gods; and people have always wanted to please, or at least appease, these gods. Most people have a sense of God within them. They have an inner feeling that there is something out there which is greater than they are. In fact, it could be said that all people have a God-shaped space within them which is crying out to God to be filled. However, although people seem to know this instinctively, they often still resist God. Why should this be?

The main reason could be that people realise their lives would have to change once they accept the presence of God. The truth is that God exists whether or not people choose to believe in Him. However, once we choose to accept His existence, it demands a response from us. We would have to recognise that we are accountable to such a God, and that really we should live our lives in the way that He chooses rather than just doing as we please. Many people do not want to accept this. For them, it's not so much a case of 'I cannot believe', as 'I do not want to believe!'

If there is a God, what is He like?

We can say that we know God exists, although we cannot see Him, by the manifestations of Him around us. But how do we know what He is like? There are a number of ways of finding out.

We can look at what He has created, because something of the creator is always revealed in whatever he creates (just like something of the painter is revealed in his paintings). If the world around us was created by God, then we would expect it to reveal something of the God who created it. We can see, then, that God must like variety, contrast, beauty, colour, and be interested in the tiniest of details. Think of the beautiful pattern you see when a snowflake is magnified, and there is a different pattern for every one! Look at a majestic sunset or the detailed plumage of a peacock, smell the perfume of a full-blown rose, or just stop and wonder at the intricacies of human birth.

We can look at what He has inspired to be written, ie, the Bible. In this, God tells us much about Himself—that He loves us; He is willing to forgive; He is merciful; He is holy; He cannot tolerate sin or rebellion; He knows everything that is going on and He is in control; He is all-powerful; and He is too big for us to fully understand with our limited minds. Read it for yourself and see!

We can look to God ourselves. God may be too big for us to fully understand, but the Bible tells us that if we draw near to Him, then He will draw near to us. We need to make a point of seeking after Him if He really is there. The best way to get to know a person is to develop a relationship with them. The same is true between us and God.

God decided to show us what He is like by coming to the earth. God's name while He was here was Jesus. Jesus, Himself, said, 'He who has seen me has seen the Father.'

What is atheistic philosophy?

An atheist is a person who does not believe in the existence of God or gods. A philosopher is someone who loves the study and pursuit of wisdom and knowledge, especially that which deals with 'ultimate reality'. Many people in the world today (including a majority of political leaders) are atheistic philosophers, although they may not call themselves this. They prefer not to bother with God. In fact, they deny His existence. Instead, they try to work out a meaning to life without bringing God into it. They say that the purpose of life is to do as much as you possibly can within it, because at the end there is nothing. Death is extinction! They believe that human beings are totally responsible for their own good or evil. Everything that happens is due to either human effort, natural causes, or chance.

The trouble with this kind of reasoning is that although it is logical, it is empty. Surely there is more to life than just living and making the best of what we have! Why do we have a conscience which tells us what is right and what is not? Does it matter what we do? If there is no accountability, then we may as well do what we want, as long as we can get away with it! If there is nothing at the end, does anything really matter? Most people know deep down that there is more to life than this.

What about the other religions?

Many people believe that all religions lead to the same God and, therefore, it doesn't matter which one you choose as long as you are sincere. In the Western world today, we pride ourselves on our tolerance and we want to believe that God, if He exists, is also tolerant. The trouble with this type of reasoning is that it leaves God out. It is us deciding that God should be like ourselves, instead of our finding out what God wants.

All religions cannot be right, since most of them are contradictory and certainly all of them say vastly different things. So which is right? Let's take a brief look at some of the other religions and their view of God.

Hinduism

Hindus practise meditation. Through it they try to relax, forget about the world and its problems, and come closer to their impersonal gods. The process is helped by the bodily exercises of yoga. They have a very fatalistic approach to life. In fact, they blame everything on the whims of their gods, or on something that they have done to please or displease these gods.

Buddhism

Buddhists do not have a personal or creator God to believe in. They believe that people have within themselves the capacity for their own salvation. They see the body as full of evil, but believe it can be overcome by acts of self-denial and self-discipline. This is the only way of reaching the state of eternal bliss—Nirvana. The Buddhist sees life as a continual quest for Nirvana. They also believe in reincarnation, which allows them to continue their quest over many lifetimes. In Buddhism, the level you managed to achieve during your lifetime determines your reincarnated state, ie, whether you have progressed or gone backwards in your quest for eternal bliss. It supposedly took Buddha 547 births to reach Nirvana.

Islam

Muslims stress total obedience to an interpretation of their holy book, the Koran, in order to please God. They believe that you need to work at pleasing God—the harder you work, the more chance of success you have. Fear of not being good enough pervades this religion, because its followers do not know the God of love or forgiveness. There are also many other religions, such as Confucianism, Bahai, Taoism, and animism, etc. It is not the purpose of this book to go through all of these; suffice it to say that Christianity is unique in its message and in the effect it has on its true followers.

Why is Christianity different?

Unlike Christians, followers of other religions do not claim a personal knowledge of God. In fact, they have no certainty at all that their remote and impersonal God will accept them. These religions all stress that the only thing to do in life is to try to improve, to try to obey the moral and religious rules, and to hope that this is enough to merit God's forgiveness and eternal life. Do you think you could ever be good enough, of yourself, to be accepted by a perfect God?

Christianity, however, is different. It is founded by Jesus, who didn't just come as a prophet or messenger of God, who pointed the way to Him—He claimed to be God! He said that He was the way, the truth and the life and that no one could come to God the Father but by Him. Jesus promised complete forgiveness for everything we do which displeases God and eternal life to all who would follow Him.

True Christianity is trusting in Jesus and what He did for

us, rather than trusting in our own good deeds to bring us to God and merit His favour. Unlike other religions, Christianity offers a personal relationship with God. The Bible even teaches that Christians have a part of God, Himself, called the Holy Spirit, who has come to live in them and help them to live in a way which pleases God.

3

Who Was Jesus
And What Did He Do?

Did Jesus exist or is He a myth?

We know that Jesus did exist nearly 2,000 years ago. We can be sure of this, because a number of non-Christian writers mentioned Jesus in their writings. Two famous Roman writers of the period tell us about Him, ie, Tacitus (Annals 15.44) and Pliny the Younger (Letters 10.96); and so do two Jewish writings, ie, the writings of Josephus (especially Antiquities 18.33) and the Mishnah. These texts were written by people who were not involved in Christianity, yet they tell us that: Jesus was an historical figure; He had an unusual birth; He did do miracles; He did teach as the Bible suggests; He did have disciples; He did claim to be the Messiah; He died by crucifixion; resurrection was claimed; and He promised to return at the end of history.

What did Jesus say about Himself?

Jesus taught and lived by the highest moral standards known to humankind. Most people who know His teachings accept that they are remarkable. Yet Jesus was more than just a moral teacher. The Bible shows us that Jesus claimed: He could forgive people their sins; He had a right to people's worship; He alone represented the way to God; He was the truth; He embodied the life of God; He came to seek out and save the lost; He could give peace to everyone who came to Him; He would give His life as a ransom for many; He would rise from the dead; and on Judgement Day, all humanity will be accountable to Him.

Jesus backed up His claims by knowing what was in people's hearts, by repeatedly doing miracles, and finally by being raised from the dead.

Did Jesus really die and then rise from the dead?

When the Romans executed someone, they made sure that person was dead before they removed them from the cross. In Jesus' case, they made doubly sure by sticking a spear into His side. When they did this, a mixture of water and blood came pouring out—a sure medical sign of death. Jesus' friends who took His body off the cross were convinced of His death. They would not have laid His body in a tomb, rolled a stone over the entrance, and then allowed it to be sealed, if they thought He was still alive. Neither would they have arrived a couple of days later with spices to anoint His body, if they knew He was alive.

What happened to Jesus' body after He died?

Three alternatives have been put forward:

1 The Jewish or Roman authorities took the body. If they had, they would have certainly produced it when the friends of Jesus started to claim He was risen and alive.

2 Jesus' friends took the body. This would mean that they would have had to either overpower or bribe the soldiers assigned to guard the tomb, and there is no evidence of this. In fact, the disciples were so demoralised and scared at this point, that it is hard to imagine them doing anything like this. Finally, there is no way that the disciples would have later risked their lives proclaiming that Jesus was alive, if they knew all along that this was a lie.

3 God raised Jesus from the dead. Many people claim to have seen Jesus after His death. Sometimes, He appeared to an individual, but at other times He showed Himself to a small group of people or a crowd. The claim to have seen Jesus, therefore, cannot be explained away as an hallucination or mob hysteria. Jesus, knowing the questions that would be raised by humankind, proved that He was not a ghost by allowing His friends to touch Him. He even ate with them!

There was also an incredible transformation in the disciples, themselves. At the time of Jesus' death, they were scared, disillusioned, broken people. After they claimed He had risen from the dead, they became bold, confident people. Fearlessly, they proclaimed that Jesus had risen from the dead, that He was alive, and that people could encounter Him for themselves. These same disciples ended up turning the then known world upside-down for God with this message. And it didn't end there! Throughout history, millions of people claim to have had an encounter with Jesus for themselves and have had changed lives as a result—and the same thing is happening today!

What does the Bible say Jesus did for us?

The Bible teaches us that when Jesus came to the earth, He achieved a great deal for every person who has ever lived.

He showed us the love of God. The love of God for us is beyond human understanding. It is not mere friendship, affection or loyalty, it is the sacrificial and unconditional love of God, who gave Himself completely to save His creation, ie, you and me! In fact, God loves us so much, that if we put our trust in His Son Jesus, He has promised to

17

provide us with everything we need to live a fulfilled life, not just now, but for eternity.

He made forgiveness possible and so delivered us from God's judgement. Jesus took everything that we have done to displease God (which we can call sin) into Himself. He took the full weight of the anger of God which was caused by our sin, and He bore it in Himself on the cross on which He died. Jesus didn't become a sinner, He became our sin! To get the benefit of this incredible gift from God, we need to put our trust in Jesus. Those who trust in Him need fear no judgement from God, because Jesus has already taken the punishment. Sin also disrupts our conscience and causes the feelings of guilt and the lack of real peace which most of us know. Therefore, by taking the punishment for our sin, Jesus has provided the way for us to be free of our feelings of guilt.

He made a way for us to have a restored relationship with God. According to the Bible, human beings originally had a good relationship with God. This was spoilt when we chose to do our own thing instead of obeying God. This decision separated us from God and it created a barrier between us and Him. As a result, it seems to us that God is either far away or not there at all. Jesus, however, made a way through that barrier, enabling us to have a relationship with God again.

He rescued us from death. Fear of death is the root cause of most, if not all, fear. Death holds no fear for the Christian, because their trust is in Jesus, who overcame death and broke its power when He was raised from the dead.

He understands us. Jesus was fully human and yet He was also fully God. He became human in order to experience the sort of problems which we face here on earth. He, therefore, knows what we need to enable us to deal with the problems and difficulties we face in life.

What should our response to Jesus be?

If Jesus is who He claimed to be, then He is the most important person in history. He claimed to be the Son of God, the Christ or Messiah, who came into the world to rescue every person who has ever lived. Other people may have made such claims, but none have lived a life like Jesus or made the impact on the world that He has.

If Jesus wasn't who He claimed to be, then He must have either been mad or a con-man. That would mean that millons of people throughout history have been fooled and even given up their lives for a lie. However, history itself has been changed by this man, and about one-third of the world's population today at least nominally follow Him. In fact, millions of people claim to know Him personally and they live their lives under His guidance and direction. This man, who lacked higher education and who was only a carpenter by trade, has had more influence on humanity than any other person in history. If He was a liar or a lunatic, He made quite an impact!

If Jesus is who He claims—if He did die, was raised from the dead, and went to be with His Father in heaven—then He is alive today and we ignore Him at our peril.

Could He be the vital ingredient your life is missing? Is He the piece of the jigsaw of life that makes sense of all the other pieces?

4

What Is True Christianity?

What Christianity isn't

Being a true Christian is not a case of being born in a Christian country or into a Christian family. It is not being a good person, doing good deeds, or living by high moral standards. It is not going to a Christian church on a regular basis. Neither is it believing in God or reading the Bible. It is not even being confirmed or baptised, either as an infant or as an adult.

What is true Christianity?

The heart of Christianity is God so loving us that He sent His Son, Jesus, to find us and bring us into a close and loving relationship with Him, both now in this life, and throughout the whole of eternity. Jesus said of Himself that He was the way, the truth and the life, and that no one comes to God but by Him. True Christianity is putting our trust in Jesus and what He did for us, and then following after Him. It answers the deep questions of life, because all of us here on earth have been designed by God to know Him and enjoy a relationship with Him for ever.

What is the true church?

The church of God is not a building (although Christians may meet in a church building), and it is not a sect or denomination—Catholic or Protestant. The true church of God is the family of people who belong to Him here on earth. It is the great world-wide body of people, whatever their colour, wealth, background or intellect, who trust and follow Jesus.

There are differences in the way in which local groups of true Christians (ie, local churches) express their relationship with God. In fact, this is one of the main reasons why we have the various church denominations that we do, eg, Anglican, Baptist, Pentecostal, Free Church, etc. However, if the people who make up a local church truly are an expression of Jesus' world-wide body of true Christians, then it does not particularly matter about the form of structure of that church and its services. The only really important thing about any church is that God is able to do what He wants to do with that group of people.

Note: God will have a particular local church that He wants any true Christian to attend. This church will be just what that person needs.

Why is the church so irrelevant, boring and old-fashioned?

Unfortunately, many local churches today are irrelevant, boring, and old-fashioned. However, this is not what God intended for His church.

The Bible reveals to us what God's church should be like. It should be a loving, caring community of Christians, who not only look after and love each other, but who also reach out to the world and present to it the life of God. The church is God's chosen agency to carry on the work which Jesus began. In fact, it should be the expression of Jesus on earth today. The Christian church should therefore be a dynamic, relevant, life-changing organisation.

The good news is that some local churches today are more like God's ideal. These churches may not be perfect, but they are attempting to live up to the Bible's image of what the Christian church should be like.

Why is there so much hypocrisy in the church?

Things have not changed much since Jesus' day. He found a great deal of hypocrisy in the religious organisations of His time. Jesus' response to hypocrisy is as relevant today as it was then. He told the hypocrites to stop their hypocrisy, get their lives right with God, and then serve Him whole-heartedly. This is the way things should be in God's church today.

Isn't Christianity just a crutch for the weak?

Many people today like to think of themselves as strong and independent. They do all right on their own, so why do they need God? It is easy for such people to despise Christianity. In fact, they often reduce Christianity to the level of being merely a crutch for the weak. In one sense, they are right! True Christians know their need of God and just how dependent on Him they really are.

The truth is that our society is full of crutches. In fact, we depend on them. Some of these, like drugs and alcohol, actually do us damage. Most crutches, however, are simply harmless things upon which we rely. For example, when we are sick, we rely on doctors, medicine and hospitals; employers rely on their employees and vice versa; and marriage partners rely on each other. To say that we do not have (and need) any crutches on which we depend, is naive to say the least. True Christians know they are needy people. They know that they cannot get on in life without God and everything He does for them.

Note: if you are going to take Christianity seriously and follow God wholeheartedly, it is not an easy option. In fact, it takes a great deal of strength to live a true Christian life. Christians have often been cruelly persecuted for their faith. Many Christians throughout history have been brutally tortured and some have even lost their lives, simply because they have refused to renounce their Christianity. They could have so easily avoided such a fate, but they would not. They realised that they had discovered something which was far more important than life itself.

However, it isn't all bad news. Even in their difficulty, these people knew the strength of God helping them through. In fact, God promises to provide all Christians with everything they need in order to serve Him, no matter how difficult or demanding things get. He also promises to give every Christian a full and abundant life.

Don't people become Christians through social conditioning?

If this is true, why are so many people becoming Christians in Third World countries, ie, countries which are not so-called 'Christian' countries? The truth is that many people are responding to Jesus even though they are hearing about Him, and what He has done for them, for the first time. In fact, many of these people have to put up with state and family persecution because they become Christians.

On the other hand, in many 'Christian' countries, people are rebelling against so-called Christian beliefs being forced onto them. True Christianity is certainly not a result of social conditioning. People have to decide for themselves whether or not they are going to accept the claims of Jesus and follow after Him.

Doesn't Christianity stifle personal freedom?

What is freedom? Is it a licence to do what we want when we feel like it, or is it having the option to do what we want? Are we always qualified to know what is best for us, or has history proved that often, when mankind thinks it has discovered something that will allow freedom, it really has the opposite effect?

Many people think of God as a heavy authority who wants them to live by a set of boring, restrictive rules. They believe that God wants to mess up their lives and take away their personal freedom. The reason for this is that they are basically selfish at heart. They would rather go their own way than have God's way (or anyone else's) imposed on them. The truth is that none of us are ever really free. We are all bound to some degree by our society and the expectations of other people. In fact, many of us are bound by more basic things like mortgages, debt, or the need to earn enough money to live. Others of us are bound by loneliness and hopelessness. Christianity may have rules to live by, but it also provides answers to life's questions and gives life purpose and meaning.

Unfortunately, many Christians impose false rules upon themselves and others around them. These rules are usually petty and stupid, and are often contrary to Bible teaching. Do not be put off by these. God will show you what He actually requires you to do for Him, as you read the Bible, listen to your conscience, and listen to what other, more mature, Christians have to say. The Bible says that God's burden is easy and His yoke is light. He is not going to make it too difficult for us to follow Him. Remember, He has promised to help us through the inevitable difficulties of life, if we continue to look to and follow after Him. In fact, whatever the circumstances, God has promised to provide every Christian with everything they need.

If God really did create us, if He really did know us before we were born, and He does only want the best for us, as the Bible suggests, then who is more qualified than He to grant us true freedom? He knows us better than we know ourselves! It is this God who promises us an abundant life, and freedom from hopelessness and emptiness, if we seek after and follow Him. Perhaps He is the purpose your life is missing at the moment?

Remember, though, Christianity is not an easy option. It is not something which will take away all our troubles. In fact, it might add a few! What Christianity does claim is that it is the answer to the puzzle of life. It gives our life meaning by releasing us to know God and His purposes for us. This is true freedom. After all, as we have seen, if God really did create us, then He will know what we need and what is best for us, better than we do ourselves. When you read about Jesus, doesn't He seem to be a remarkably free person? And yet He lived only to do the will of God! True Christians should also live only to do the will of God. However, instead of leading them into bondage, this brings them into a true and lasting personal freedom.

Aren't Christians too other-worldly to be of any earthly use?

Throughout history, Christians, who on the surface may seem to have their heads in the clouds, have made a dynamic impact on the world. This is not surprising! After all, if there really is a God who is interested in humanity, then you would expect those who follow Him to make an impact. Some modern examples of this are Mother Teresa, Martin Luther King, and Billy Graham.

True Christians should be concerned for the world and its needs, for the simple reason that they know God shares that concern. He proved it by paying the ultimate price. He sent His Son Jesus into the world to suffer and die at the hands of sinful men, so that everyone could have the opportunity of knowing Him. He got involved, and He wants His followers to get involved. After all, Christians are supposed to be His ambassadors on earth. They should be bringing the life and light of Jesus to all who need it.

God has provided a way and a hope for all people, but we must choose whether we will accept it and go His way, or reject it and go our own way. The choice is ours!

5

What About Evolution?

Are there only two possibilities?

There are only two possible explanations for the world as we know it—divine creation or evolution. Evolution is the theory that all the living things which we find in the world today have developed from one simple ancestor over many millions of years. Most people accept evolution as fact, even though it is unprovable, because the only alternative is to believe that there is/are higher being/s who had a hand in creating the world and everything in it.

The purpose of this next chapter is not to try to prove that God created the world (because it is not possible to do this with the knowledge we have), but to show that the theory of evolution is just as unprovable.

Is evolution a mathematical improbability?

George Gallup, the statistician, once said, 'I could prove God statistically. Take the human body alone—the chance that all the functions of the individual would just happen is a statistical monstrosity.'

Only a lunatic would believe that a motor car could just form by itself given enough time and all the right materials being present. Yet there are intelligent, highly educated, professional people who tell us that the entire universe came into being by chance; that there was really no higher intelligence at work on it. The world we live in is a complicated masterpiece. In ideal conditions, everything is balanced perfectly. The human body alone is an absolute miracle. Could all this just happen by chance?

To believe that unaided dead matter produced life, that living matter produced a brain, that a brain produced reason and a conscience, and that the chaos of chance produced the cosmos of order as we see it in nature, seems to call for more faith than Christianity ever does.

Is evolution contrary to physical laws?

One of the most accepted laws of science states that everything is running down and moving towards greater disorder. The evolutionist, who does not believe in God or any other 'higher intelligence', has no answer to this problem. The evolutionist claims that without any external help, order gradually came into being out of the original disorder or chaos. The truth is that all living organisms require a 'motor' to enable them to bring order out of disorder. For example, plant cells use energy from the sun to enable them to bring order (manufacture complex carbohydrates) out of disorder (carbon dioxide and water). They can do this because they have a 'motor', known as photosynthesis. Evolutionists have no answer as to how these 'motors' first formed. In fact, even evolution itself requires a 'motor' to enable it to occur and evolutionists cannot provide any evidence to show that this 'evolutionary motor' exists.

All this suggests that the world itself is the product of intelligent being/s who is/are outside of the created order found here. The Bible states that it was God who created the order we now see from the chaos which existed.

What about fossils?

Evolutionists say that the most positive evidence for evolution is fossils. Geologists tell us that the older rocks on earth contain the simplest fossils, while the newer ones contain the most complicated, and thus the more complicated things have evolved from the simpler. This sounds simple and logical, but there are many flaws in this reasoning.

Firstly, there can be no degree of accuracy as to when prehistoric rocks were formed. Even radiometric dating, which is used to date rocks formed by volcanic activity, may be charged with being inaccurate. In fact, it would be difficult to find one rock (or fossil) where everyone accepts the age determined by a specific radiometric dating method. Rocks which we can date accurately and uncritically, do not encourage us to accept the results of radiometric dating. In one notable case, a rock was dated by the uranium decay and potassium-argon methods and it was shown to be 160 million years old, when the truth is that it was actually produced by a volcanic eruption in 1801.

Secondly, evolutionists claim that all living things developed from one simple ancestor, becoming progressively more complex as time went on. For this to be true, the fossil record should show simple creatures gradually changing to become more complex ones. If this progression did occur, we would expect to find many fossil 'links' (or transitional forms) between the different sorts of creatures that have existed (or still exist today). For evolution to be true, there should not be just one link, but thousands of them. In fact, the fossil record should be full of them. However, in reality there is not even one! Oh, a few are claimed and are written about in textbooks (eg, the horse), but examination of these so-called links has shown that the fossil animals were probably unrelated to each other. It is true that different animal species adapt to their environment and this contributes to the incredible variety that exists in the living world, but there is no proof that one species is changing to become another more complex one, even over millions of years.

Has evolution made some false claims?

Some of the support for evolution has regrettably come from falsified evidence. For example, at one point, evolutionists thought that more complex animals followed out their evolutionary descent in their development before birth. One biologist of the time has been shown to have forged some of his drawings of foetuses to support the theory.

Perhaps the most striking hoaxes have been in the field of the evolution of man from the apes. Many missing links were supposedly found and written about in textbooks. Some of these include: Piltdown man, Java man and Pekin man; all of which are known today to be either forgeries (ie, skulls made from human and animal bones put together and made to look old) or bones which were found in places where other normal human bones were also found (indicating that the skull was probably just a human deformity or that some other animal was buried in the same place).

Are there any alternatives to evolution for the person who does not believe in God or any other higher intelligence?

For many people evolution has to be true, because the only alternative to it is to believe that some other higher being/s exist/s and he/they had a hand in creation. This often causes people to accept evolution blindly, even when it does not always have much concrete evidence to back it up. It also causes the evolutionists themselves to ignore even well documented contradictory evidence. These people fall into the trap of looking for and therefore only finding that which they want to find.

How then can we explain the rocks on earth which have fossils in them? Well, perhaps they are evidence of the one, total, catastrophic destruction of the earth of which the Bible speaks, when God sent a flood to destroy every air-breathing creature here on earth.

So what does this prove?

Evolution is not the fact that many people think it is. In fact, there is as much evidence for God creating the universe as there is for evolution being the answer to the mystery of creation. Science is not in conflict with the Christian faith, although evolution may be, and certainly some scientists are! In fact, many scientists are passionately committed Christians, just like people in any other walk of life.

It must also be remembered that the Bible is not a science book and therefore it is not written in scientific language. The Bible is written to reveal God to humanity, to show His dealing with humankind, and uncover His purposes for us. To try and read it as a scientific textbook will be to miss the point of the book altogether. Nevertheless, the Bible does claim to give us a history of our origins, and this clearly identifies God as creator of the universe and of human beings in particular.

6

Other Difficult Questions

Can we trust the Bible?

The Bible claims to be direct revelation from God. In it, God tells us about Himself and what He has purposed for us as His creation. It was written by at least forty different writers from all walks of life, in at least three different languages. It was also written in many different countries over a period of 1,600 years, and yet it still manages to stay consistent within itself. The same view of God is presented from beginning to end; the same insight into human nature is revealed; a common perspective of Jesus Christ runs right through the book; and the same hope in God is offered.

The Old Testament is by far the oldest part of the Bible. It seems to have changed little over the centuries because of the way it was copied. A team of people, called the scribes, used to sit and copy every letter exactly and this would then be checked thoroughly. This copying method was so accurate and successful that when some very old manuscripts were found (called the Dead Sea Scrolls), which are over 1,000 years older than any Hebrew manuscript known in recent times, much of it was found to be almost identical to our modern translations.

The New Testament is even more reliable. In fact, it is without doubt the most reliable ancient manuscript in existence (see table 1). We have today so many manuscripts of the New Testament, written so near the events themselves, that we can be sure of having a correct text (the differences are not more than minor ones). Also, the books of the New Testament were written no later than seventy years after the death of Jesus. Therefore, there would have been many people who witnessed the events surrounding the life and death of Jesus who would have been alive at the time these books were written. If the early church writings were false, then there would have undoubtedly been evidence of challenges to their authenticity, and this is not the case. In fact, even non-Christian writings of the time confirm New Testament writings.

Ancient Writing	The History of Theoydides	Caesar's Gallic War	Tacitus Histories	The Four Gospels
A) Original document writers	460-440 BC	58-50 BC	Approx. AD 100	AD 65-90
B) Oldest surviving copy	AD 900 (+ few first-century fragments)	AD 850	AD 800	AD 350 (even earlier for fragments)
C) Approx. time between A and B	1,300 years (fragments—400 years)	900 years	700 years	300 years (fragments—50 years)
D) Number of copies in existence today	8	10	4	Up to 2,000

Table 1

The Bible as a whole has been the subject of centuries of scholarly criticism, with each detail minutely examined, and yet it still stands as a credible, reliable book. Also, no archaeological discovery has cast any doubt on the truth of the Bible record.

Probably the greatest evidence of the Bible's authenticity is the effect which its writings have had on the lives of countless millions of people throughout history. If the Bible is indeed inspired by God, then this is what you would expect.

Who made God?

When we as human beings try to understand God, we run into a huge difficulty. We, with our finite minds, are trying to understand the truth about an infinite, almighty, all-powerful God who created everything. We, who are trapped in time, are attempting to know a God who has no beginning or end, and who is outside of time and therefore not limited by it. How can people, who are born and later die, understand a God who was and is and always will be?

The answer then to this question is that no one made God. He has always been and He will always be, unchanging, never decaying, and never growing old or weak.

Why is there so much suffering in the world?

The world has much within it that is good. However, this has to be balanced against the suffering and evil that we can also see. People often ask why God allows this. However, a better question to ask is, 'What are we like as people?' Most of us have to admit that we are very selfish people. We want to do our own thing. Oh, this may involve doing good to other people at times, but most of us want to get more and more for ourselves. The Bible states that people sow what they reap. When you realise what is in your heart, and you are probably not the worst person that you know, is it any wonder that the world is in such a mess?

The Bible asserts that God created a perfect world. The problems all started when the human race used its free will to decide to go its own way instead of going God's way. The Bible calls this sin and it separated us from God. Unfortunately, sin still acts as a barrier between us and God, making God seem distant, when in reality He is there to be found by us all. God still loves us as His creation, but, because He is holy, He cannot continue any form of relationship with us who have deliberately chosen to disobey Him and go our own way. Therefore, we have a world today where rebellion against God is the normal state of affairs and where the enemy of God, the devil or Satan, rules. Is it any wonder that the world is in such a mess?

There is a war between the forces of good and evil, and we are caught up in that war every day. This war leaves us with casualties and it is the reason for sickness, infirmity, disability, and handicap. Even the fabric of the world itself is caught in the conflict resulting in earthquakes, floods, hurricanes, and the like.

You may ask the question, 'If God loves us so much, why doesn't He wipe out all the evil and suffering?' The reason for this is very simple. God does want to remove all evil, but to do so would mean He would have to judge all sin and evil in humankind. If He did this, most of us would not escape punishment. Who among us is free from wrongdoing and evil? In fact, it is because God loves us so much that He is holding back that day, so that as many people as possible will be with Him for eternity.

The Bible declares that God wants none of us to perish. In fact, He wants all of us to share eternal life with Him. The only way that this is possible is through the work of Jesus. We all need to avail ourselves of God's great provision in Jesus. This is the only way that we can get out from under the domination of sin and the devil. It is possible through Jesus to be right with God and to live a victorious, fulfilled life, knowing peace with God and the God of peace.

Why does God care about this little world of ours, when we compare it with the vastness of the universe?

When we realise the vast distances of space and the millions of stars and planets within the universe, it is hard to imagine why a God, who created it all, would be interested in such an insignificant speck as the earth, let alone the people on it. The Bible says that this is the case and millions of people claim that they have a personal relationship with God to prove it. Also, when we look down a microscope, another world is revealed. A drop of water can teem with microscopic life. Even an atom is a world in itself. If God created details like this in our world, why wouldn't He be interested in our small planet in the midst of such a vast universe?

Isn't just being good, enough for God?

Living a good life is not the way to win God's favour. That would be like saying to God, 'Your Son, Jesus, was not good enough. Only my efforts to be a good person are sufficient to win your favour!' Sounds stupid doesn't it, but this is what millions of people have kidded themselves into believing. We cannot make up the rules—that's God's job. He has said in the Bible that the only way to come to Him is by turning from going our own way, accepting His Son, Jesus Christ, as our Lord and Saviour, and going His way instead. Charity, good morals, and living a good life are all very good things, but they do not satisfy God. He has only one way for humankind to come to Him, and that way is Jesus.

What happens to people who die without hearing about Jesus?

The Bible is not one hundred per cent clear on this subject, so it would be wrong to suggest that it is. However, the Bible does infer that God will judge those people who go against that which they know to be right and He will judge people according to the amount of truth they know. It also says that what may be known about God is plain to all, because God has revealed Himself—both His power and His nature—in His creation. Therefore, humankind is without excuse.

Some of you may be thinking that this is all right for reasoning adults, but what about children or the mentally handicapped? The only answer I can honestly give is that God is a God of justice, love and mercy. He will judge these people fairly, because to do otherwise would be to deny His very own nature. We can trust God with these people and know that He will do the right thing.

Why did God make us capable of disobeying Him?

Why did God let us get into this mess in the first place, if He knew what disobeying Him would do? The only way God could have done this would have been to make us without the ability to choose. This would mean that we would be little more than robots, who have to obey their creator. God wants the satisfaction and joy of knowing that we freely choose to do what He wants us to do. He wants us to freely give our love and devotion to Him. He does not want puppets who mechanically serve Him. Instead, He created us with the power to choose whether to obey, defy or ignore Him. It's our choice!

Why did God allow evil to come into existence?

This again is a difficult question to answer, because the Bible gives us no specific reason. However, it does say that evil has its source in a being called Satan. Satan, who was originally called Lucifer, was an angel of great power. He was full of wisdom and perfect in beauty. In fact, he was created as the model of perfection. He was God's blameless guardian cherub and he walked with God. Unfortunately, Lucifer became proud on account of his beauty, and corrupt because of his wisdom and splendour. He wanted, not just to do God's will and so bring glory to God, but to do his own thing and take the glory for himself. He wanted to be like or even greater than God. This caused him to become progressively more warped, so that eventually, this once marvellous creation became the source of all evil. He is now called: the father of lies, a murderer, a deceiver, and the accuser—a far cry from what he was originally.

God seems to have created Lucifer with some freedom of choice. He didn't want to create a machine which would automatically have to serve Him, but rather He wanted a being who would choose to love and obey Him. However, Lucifer chose to go his own way and so brought evil into existence. The same choice is available to us today—to choose to go God's way or our own.

7

How Do I Become A True Christian?

Why let the questions blind you?

If it is true that God created us to have a relationship with Him, then we need to work towards this throughout our lives. After all, if there really is an all-powerful creator God, then most of us would want to get to know Him (if this were possible) and do what He wants us to do. Don't let the questions looked at in previous chapters blind you to the truth as it has been revealed in Jesus. God has promised in Jesus to fill the God-shaped void in our lives. In Jesus, we can have an eternal hope and a God-based future, instead of hopelessness and emptiness. God does love us. He has proved this by sending His Son, Jesus, to make a way for us to have a relationship with Him. He doesn't want us to fail. In fact, He wants to give us an abundant, fulfilled and fruitful life. However, we can only have this when we stop doing what we want and we start living the life that He wants us to live.

What is the problem?

God created a beautiful world. It was His plan that human-kind would serve and worship Him eternally on that world. However, this plan was ruined by everyone from the first people until you and me. We have all rebelled against God.

Instead, we have chosen to live as we please, without Him. The Bible calls this sin. Because of this, the human race has been spoiled, bringing chaos and disaster into the world.

Our self-centredness and sinfulness has cut us off from God. He therefore seems to be a million miles away and disinterested in us. This has occurred because our sinfulness (doing what we want instead of what God wants) acts as a barrier between us and God. We cannot break through that barrier on our own because we are not good enough. Charity, good works, high moral standards, philosophy, and even religion, although they may be very praiseworthy (at times), all fall short of what God requires in order for us to have a relationship with Him.

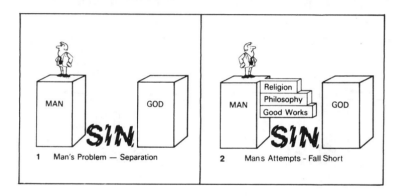

1   Man's Problem — Separation

2   Mans Attempts - Fall Short

What is God's answer?

God's answer is Jesus. Jesus is proof that God loves us and that He cares enough about us not to leave us struggling here on earth.

> *For God so loved the world* [that includes you!] *that he gave his one and only Son, that whoever believes in him shall not perish but have eternal life.*   (John 3:16)

We deserve to suffer the consequences of our sin and rejection of God, which is to be rejected by God for ever. However, God loves the world (you and me!) so much that He sent His Son, Jesus, who was also God, to share our life and hardships. But unlike us, Jesus did not sin. In fact, He went about reversing the effects of our rebellion. God's anger for our rebellion fell on Jesus, who was perfectly innocent. He was punished instead of us and died an agonising death in our place. The Bible says that when Jesus was crucified, He took our sinfulness into Himself. Jesus did not stay dead though. God raised Him from the dead and He appeared to many people here on earth before God took Him up to be with Himself. Jesus' life, death and resurrection opened the way for us to have a restored relationship with God.

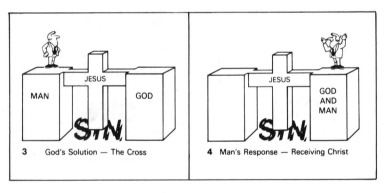

3   God's Solution — The Cross   4   Man's Response — Receiving Christ

There is nothing to stop anyone from coming to know God, no matter who they are or what they may have done. The way is wide open. God has done His part in Jesus—it is now up to us!

What is the cost of following Jesus?

If you become a true Christian, from then on Jesus should be Lord of your life. This means that Jesus should be boss of every part of your life—your work, your friendships, your family, your time, your money, etc. You should no longer live life just as you please. In fact, everything you are and have should come under His control.

Jesus did not promise that it would be easy to follow Him. In fact, if you become a true Christian, then people may misunderstand you, others may laugh at you, and others still may oppose you. Jesus Himself had to put up with these things. He knows what it is like to be human and to be rejected. However, He has also promised to give everybody who follows Him everything they need both for now, here on earth, and for eternity. Jesus said:

> *I have come that they may have life, and have it to the full.* (John 10:10)

God wants to come and live in your heart, sharing your problems, your joys, your difficulties, and sharing His Holy Spirit power to help you live life the way He intended. Jesus said:

> *I am the way and the truth and the life. No one comes to the Father* [ie, God] *except through me.* (John 14:6)

What is your response?

There are four simple steps that you need to make in order to take hold of the work Jesus did for you:

First, you need to admit that you do displease God (ie, sin) and fall short of His standards. In fact, you need to be truly sorry that you have ignored God and gone your own way.

Second, you need, with God's help, to turn from going your own way and go His way instead (ie, repent). In fact, you need to willingly turn from every thought, word, action and habit that you know is wrong. God will give you the strength to do this if you trust in Him.

Third, you need to believe that Jesus Christ, God's Son, died on a cross to take the punishment for your sin and therefore enabled you to have a relationship with God.

Fourth, you need to believe that God raised Jesus from the dead and that He is now reigning at God's right hand. You need to trust Jesus, make Him your Lord and Saviour, and commit your life to Him. To make someone Lord means that you make them boss. When Jesus asks you to do something, you need to obey Him.

Is it really this simple?

The answer is, 'Yes it is!', but only because Jesus has done all the hard work already.

> *If you confess with your mouth, 'Jesus is Lord', and believe in your heart that God raised him from the dead, you will be saved.* (Romans 10:9)

Your life is like a house. Jesus Christ is waiting outside. He will not force His way in because that is not the way of love. He wants to be invited in and only you can open the door. Jesus is waiting now for you to invite Him in. He wants to come and live in your heart and life. Don't be put off! Time is running out. Who knows what tomorrow will hold?

If you want to become a Christian and know Jesus in your life, if you want to know that all your sins are forgiven by God, if you want to know God's acceptance, become one of His children and therefore be part of His family; and if you want to have eternal life and the life of God in you, then pray the following prayer (it is best if you speak it out aloud):

Almighty God, it is true that I do things which fall short of your standards. I honestly want to turn from this which I now recognise as sin. I ask your forgiveness for all I have done that is wrong in your sight. From this moment on, I determine to go your way instead of my own way. Thank you for sending your Son, Jesus, to die on a cross so that I can be free of the punishment I deserve. I am glad that you raised Jesus from the dead and that He is alive today at your right hand in heaven. I make Jesus the Lord of my life. Please come into my heart right now so that I may be made new. Thank you for hearing my prayer. Please help me now to live the rest of my life with the help and power of the Holy Spirit which you have given to me. I pray this in Jesus' name. Amen.

Can you be sure that you are a Christian?

If you have prayed the above prayer (or another like it) and you prayed it from the heart, meaning every word, then you are a true Christian. This is the most important decision you have ever made. Whether you felt anything or not, you are changed, because God has promised this and He cannot lie. You have become a disciple or follower of Jesus. The step you have taken is only the beginning. It is like being born again and starting a new life. You are no longer on your own. You are now a child of God, and He has given you the Holy Spirit, which is part of Himself, to come and live in you. The Holy Spirit will give you all the help and power you need in order to live a life that is pleasing to God.

Just like a new-born baby has many needs in order to grow and mature, so does a new Christian. Read the next chapter to find out some of the basic things God wants you to know and do now that you are a Christian.

8

What Next?

What happened when you became a Christian?

If you have just become a Christian, then you are at the very beginning of a new life with God. At first, you may have many questions, doubts and confusions. This is hardly surprising when you realise what has just happened to you when you became a Christian. Don't worry, as you live life the way God wants you to, these questions/doubts/confusions will be answered (or dispelled) in His time. You are like a new-born child who needs to learn many things. You must also remember that you have lived life as you pleased for many years. There will therefore be many things which you need to unlearn as well.

Upon becoming a Christian, there are a number of life-changing things that have happened to you which you will need to know in order to grow and mature as a Christian. Some of the more important ones are:

You are now a child of God

> *Yet to all who received him, to those who believed in his name, he gave the right to become children of God— children born not of natural descent, nor of human decision or a husband's will, but born of God.*
>
> (John 1:12,13)

You have eternal life and you will not be condemned, because you have crossed over from death to life

> [Jesus said] *I tell you the truth, whoever hears my word and believes him who sent me has eternal life and will not be condemned; he has crossed over from death to life.* (John 5:24)

God will never leave you or forsake you

> *Keep your lives free from the love of money and be content with what you have, because God has said, 'Never will I leave you; never will I forsake you.'* (Hebrews 13:5)

You have the power available to overcome the world

> *For everyone born of God has overcome the world. This is the victory that has overcome the world, even our faith. Who is it that overcomes the world? Only he who believes that Jesus is the Son of God.* (1 John 5:4,5)

You have received part of God Himself, the Holy Spirit

> *And you also were included in Christ when you heard the word of truth, the gospel of your salvation. Having believed, you were marked in him with a seal, the promised Holy Spirit, who is a deposit guaranteeing our inheritance until the redemption of those who are God's possession—to the praise of his glory.* (Ephesians 1:13,14)

Before you became a Christian, you were a two-part person. You had a body and soul (consisting of will, mind and emotions). Upon becoming a Christian, you became a three-part person. You still have your body and soul, but your spirit, which once was not active, has now been made alive by the Holy Spirit. So instead of just relying on yourself and on what your five senses teach you, as you did before, you can now rely on God who is dwelling within you in the form of the Holy Spirit.

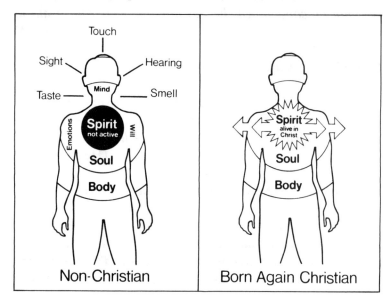

What you need to do now

The Bible is far too full of God-given, helpful instructions aimed at the Christian for me to write them all down here. We will just look at a few of the more important ones. In fact, unless you put the following principles into action in your life, you will not grow and mature as a Christian.

A Christian is a disciple or follower of Jesus. The Bible says,

> *'Whoever claims to live in him must walk as Jesus did.'*
> (1 John 2:6)

If you have just become a true Christian, from now on you should put the claims of Jesus first in your life regardless of the cost to yourself. A helpful way to do this is to ask yourself, 'What would Jesus do?' in every situation you come across. When you gave your life to God, you made Him Lord of it. That means He, not you, is boss!. You therefore need to obey everything He asks you to do. Remember, though, God is love. He will only ask you to do things which grow out of the love that He has for you and other people.

The Bible is a God-inspired book which needs to be read and studied regularly by every Christian. In the Bible, God gives important instructions on how every Christian should live. Get a version of the Bible (at least the New Testament) which you can understand. We recommend the New International Version. Read the New Testament first. In fact, a good place to start reading is the Gospel of John in the New Testament. Read at least a chapter a day. Before you start to read, ask God to show you things about Himself and things which He wants you to do for Him. Your local church should also have details of Bible reading aids which have proved helpful to many people.

All Christians need to pray to God. Prayer is simply talking with and listening to God. Praying with God on a regular basis will enable your relationship with Him to grow. God wants you to ask Him for help and He wants to reveal His will to you. You need to make room in your life for prayer. After a while, you will wonder how you ever managed in life without it.

You cannot be a Christian on your own. You are now part of God's world-wide family of believers and you should not isolate yourself from other members of that family. Christians are like coals glowing in a fire. Together, we all give warmth and light to each other, as well as to others outside the fire. But if we do not get fellowship with other Christians, we will begin to lose our fire—we will begin to go cold. You need to be in the fire together with other Christians. The best place to do this is in a local church where Jesus Christ is preached as Lord and Saviour. God will have a local church which is just right for you to attend. It will need you as much as you need it. This church should enable you to have fellowship with other Christians, grow spiritually, learn about God, worship Him, and serve Him. Without it, you will not find it easy to be a Christian. Find the church which God has for you by praying to Him about it.

The Bible teaches us to tell other people about Jesus and all He has done for us. You need to make sure that you don't keep your Christianity to yourself. God wants you to share what you have discovered with others. It is a matter of life and death for them!

Ask God to fill you with His Holy Spirit on a daily basis. You need the Holy Spirit to empower you and to enable you to serve God effectively.

And finally!

Jesus said:

> *If anyone would come after me, he must deny himself and take up his cross daily and follow me.... What good is it for a man to gain the whole world, and yet lose or forfeit his very self?* (Luke 9:23–25)

It is no good only giving God the bits of your life that you want to give Him. God wants you to follow Him wholeheartedly. In fact, you need to continually keep your eyes on Him and not let yourself be distracted from following after Him. God sent His Son Jesus to die for you, so that you might have an eternal relationship with Him. He has given your life meaning and purpose. You need to give your life totally over to Him and obey Him, knowing that He has promised to be with you always.

True Christianity is the answer to the question of life.

Glossary Of Questions

Suggested Reading
For Further Information

Field, D. and Toon, P., 'Real Questions' (Lion)

Gaukroger, S., 'It Makes Sense' (Scripture Union)

Little, P.E., 'Know Why You Believe' (Scripture Union)

Little, P.E., 'Know What You Believe' (Scripture Union)

Baker, S., 'Bone Of Contention' (Evangelical Press)

Gordon, B. and Fardouly, D., 'First Steps' (Sovereign World)

If you have enjoyed this book and would like to help us to send a copy of it and many other titles to needy pastors in the **Third World**, please write for further information or send your gift to:

Sovereign World Trust, P.O. Box 777, Tonbridge, Kent TN11 9XT, United Kingdom

or to the **'Sovereign World'** distributor in your country. If sending money from outside the United Kingdom, please send an International Money Order or Foreign Bank Draft in STERLING, drawn on a **UK** bank to **Sovereign World Trust**.